BY THE CO-AUTHOR OF THE ACCLAIMED

Sexual Abuse in America: Epidemic of the 21st Century

THE THERAPEUTIC RELATIONSHIP
IN SEX OFFENDER TREATMENT

GERAL T. BLANCHARD, M.A.

Safer Society Press

PO BOX 340 • BRANDON, VERMONT 05733

Editors: Euan Bear, Stacey Bird, Rob Freeman-Longo, and David E. Robinson
Cover Design: Barbara Poeter, Pittsford, VT

ISBN: 1-884444-15-6

$12.00

Order from:

The Safer Society Press
PO Box 340
Brandon, Vermont 05733-0340
(802) 247-3132

Acknowledgments

My sincere gratitude goes to Rob Freeman-Longo for believing in the importance of this project. To the editors, Euan, David, and Stacey, I extend my appreciation for helping make my words much more readable. Members of the Advanced Studies Group on Sexual Addiction not only contributed to the development of many of the ideas contained herein, they also served as a moral compass. Humble thanks go to the numerous Quaker prison volunteers who quietly modeled the relationship skills I described. I also want to acknowledge the good mentoring that has come from clinicians in Manitoba, Hawaii, Minnesota, and Sweden. And, finally, a deep respect is imparted to the many recovering offenders who successfully transformed their lives in my presence and, as a result, restored my faith in the human condition.

About the Author

Geral Blanchard, M.A., C.A.S., is currently a program development consultant in the field of sex offender treatment. For over 26 years he worked as a clinician treating sex offenders and their victims. In addition to his other books, *Sex Offender Treatment: A Psycho-educational Model* (1989) and *Sexual Abuse in America: Epidemic of the Twenty-First Century* (1998), Geral has authored numerous treatment manuals and professional journal articles. He lectures throughout the United States and Canada and resides in the Big Horn Mountains of Wyoming with his wife, Teri.

Contents

Foreword

TREATING PERSONS WHO sexually abuse is one of the most demanding jobs of a mental health practitioner. Traditional mental health techniques are often ineffective with this difficult-to-treat population unless combined with specialized treatment techniques and a firm, caring demeanor.

Most sex abusers are involuntary clients sent to clinicians and programs by the courts or correctional agencies such as probation and parole. Their treatment is mandatory, and their failure to successfully complete treatment can result in severe consequences, including long-term incarceration. This mandate can strain the client-therapist relationship from the beginning. Yet few professionals are trained in how to work with involuntary clients.

Sex crimes generate emotions such as fear, anger, and frustration in those who hear about them. The sex offender treatment specialist is no stranger to these feelings. Without proper guidance, supervision, training, and ongoing collegial support, professionals who treat sex offenders often face unresolved anger and stress, feelings that have a negative impact on their work and affect their ability to effectively treat their sex offender clients.

It is common for treatment professionals to begin unconsciously displacing their anger onto these difficult clients, especially when some clients minimize or deny engaging in sexually abusive acts that have traumatized other human beings. One essential coping strategy in this work is learning to separate the offense behavior from the individual offender.

Author Geral Blanchard focuses on the therapeutic relationship. He acknowledges that standard sex-offender treatment techniques can be productive in client treatment while cautioning that they may sometimes interfere with developing a positive therapeutic relationship when rigidly applied or misused.

The Difficult Connection can help professionals keep the balance between effective treatment and maintaining a positive therapeutic relationship with a sexually abusive client. It offers a new perspective on the difficulty therapists face in developing a client-therapist relationship. It demonstrates ways the professional can enhance the relationship in an effort to offer the client an opportunity to participate in a more productive and positive treatment experience. We hope you find insights and assistance in these pages, and, as always, we appreciate your work toward making society safer for all of us.

Rob Freeman-Longo
Safer Society Foundation, Inc.
Brandon, VT

Introduction

THE DIFFICULT CONNECTION: *The Therapeutic Relationship in Sex Offender Treatment* is intended to be a clarion call to therapists, reminding them of the healing power of relationship. It is this power upon which all counseling techniques depend. This book may also serve as a primer for helping professionals who are preparing for the often-arduous task of treating sex offenders.

This short work devotes little attention to the conventional forms of treatment, such as the behavioral, cognitive, and medical models. A great deal has already been written on counseling techniques that advance the recovery process. I will not attempt to duplicate that material. Instead I want to discuss the importance of overcoming the many obstacles that impede relationship-building with this specific client group — a group that evokes strong emotions in all of us.

One of the obstacles to building positive therapeutic relationships with sex offenders is an American political and emotional climate that encourages some therapists to take a punitive and shaming stance toward their sex-offending clients. While most people would agree that firm consequences are needed for sex offenders, unfortunately American culture fosters violent and vindictive attitudes that also need close examination and change. Treating sex crimes requires a broader focus than individual pathology alone. We must also identify and confront society's role in creating a climate conducive to individual aggression and subjugation.

This book also calls the reader back to some of the fundamental tenets of psychology and morality, principles that apply to all types of clients, sex offenders included. It lends support to addictionologists, who have noted the frequency with which sexual addiction accompanies sexual crimes.

The potential to exploit others sexually can be seen as a normal urge. Sex criminals are not remarkably different from "normal" men on a psychological level. Many of us entertain hateful, violent, and abusive thoughts, yet we restrain ourselves from acting on them.

In many instances, the sex criminal is very similar to those who may loathe him. We desire to see the forces of evil as lying outside of ourselves, outside of our culture. In reality, except for the minority of very violent and sadistic sex crimes, we can obtain an understanding of sex offenders by doing some fearsome and very personal soulsearching. If we do this soul-searching honestly, as individuals and as a culture, American society could find itself less prone to violence and the violent punishment of violence.

While studies conducted outside the realm of academia have proclaimed the untreatability of sex offenders, I argue the contrary. Differential diagnostic techniques can identify many types of individuals who can benefit from a therapeutic intervention when it is matched with the swift and firm application of consequences. Because so many sex offenders have experienced dysfunctional and abusive primary relationships, an essential element of restoration lies in the healing power of interpersonal relationships — particularly the relationship with the therapist. From a solid and trusting therapeutic alliance, a light of goodness — no matter how small — can be ignited.

A word of caution to the reader: In a world given to blackand-white, either-or thinking, you may be tempted to read this book looking for the "right" way or the "wrong" way to fashion a therapeutic approach. My criticism of the impersonal features of mechanical therapeutic approaches is not meant to suggest that we "throw out the baby with the bath water." The healing professions must add to their repertoire of strategies and techniques as knowledge advances. At the same time, we must not forget the proven principles of humanistic psychology that can effectively enhance science and technology. Many therapists successfully blend mechanistic techniques with a warm and dignified therapeutic presence.

Restoring sex offenders to a non-criminal lifestyle is a ministry of sorts. It requires therapists to moralize over an individual's misdeeds. It also requires each person engaged in that ministry to be squarely grounded in a foundation of caring values. Throughout the book, I have inserted quotations that offer differing perspectives on sex criminals. Some are pragmatic, others are lofty. Apply what works for you and for the clients under your care.

Finally, while it is increasingly apparent that women, children, and adolescents are perpetrating sex crimes at alarming rates, this book will directly address only the adult male perpetrator. The contents of this book, however, have across-the-board application.

Geral T. Blanchard
Sheridan, Wyoming

CHAPTER 1

Societal Responses to Sexual Offending

Mutilation is too good for these people, it should be mandatory for these creeps.
— Brad Owen, Washington State Senator
("Washington state senate OKs castration bill," 1990, p. 2)

It has always been a mystery to me how men can feel themselves honored by the humiliation of their fellow beings.
— Mahatma Gandhi
(Quoted in Larson & Micheels-Cyrus, 1987, p. 173)

FEW CRIMES AROUSE the public's vindictive passions more than sex offenses. While victim sympathy usually prompts the loud calls for revenge, some authorities believe that violent tendencies, including murderous impulses, are touched off in all of us by the men and women who commit these crimes (Strean & Freeman, 1993).

Perhaps an appropriate starting point in examining societal reactions is to look at the media's depictions of sex crimes and the public's response to them. Television and newspaper accounts repeatedly present the shock, disbelief, rage, and repulsion of citizens when a sex crime occurs close to home. The shock and disbelief escalates when well-known and highly respected community members are reported to have molested or raped someone. We like to believe that sex crimes are committed only by demented and perverted individuals living in distant places, not by people we may know in our own communities.

When Washington State Senator Brad Owen lashed out against those "creeps," he was almost certainly responding in part to the media's reporting of the sadistic mutilation and murder of a seven-year-old Tacoma boy ("Washington state senate," 1990). From that horrible event, Owen made a common mistake. Like most Americans who learn of this crime through the media, Owen wrongly assumed this was a typical sex crime and that all sex offenders could be lumped together in one stereotypical package of pathology. From that erroneous premise, one might naturally conclude that all sex offenders must be treated and/or punished in a similar manner. While some perpetrators of sex crimes can be extraordinarily violent and sadistic, it is probably more accurate to label these men as *psychopathic murderers*. Their fatal crimes may have sexual components, but such acts are not typical of the vast majority of sex crimes committed in the United States.

Senator Owen isn't alone in his thinking. *USA Today* columnist Dan Warrensford wrote about the "vermin" and "maggots" who commit sex offenses (1990, March 7). His solutions are representative of a large part of the general population. For those men and women who attempt sex crimes, Warrensford proposes life sentences in solitary confinement. Should an actual assault occur, he believes the death penalty is the only suitable punishment. When forced to consider an alternative consequence, Warrensford suggested that all sex offenders be exiled to a distant island prison where neutering — combined with lobotomies — would be performed by volunteers. Where the volunteers would come from was not specified.

One reader went even further. She suggested, in the same edition, that sex offenders should be assaulted in the same way that they assaulted others. If someone raped a child, he would be raped in the same fashion. The reader failed to say who would do her legislated raping.

We can expect emotional responses from media depictions of violent crimes. When emotions rule, logic disappears. Long-range vision vanishes. For its own comfort the public wants a response that distances it from the crime and returns suffering in kind. Sex offending seems to be seen as a distant person's individual pathology — certainly not as the cultural phenomenon it is, with roots in all of us. No wonder that a clinician can develop a less than humanistic attitude toward this group of clients when he or she is continuously exposed to the media and public opinion.

In actuality, sex crimes are usually the act of someone very familiar to the victim. The offender may be a father, teacher, coach, or pastor. That sex offending can occur so readily in traditionally sacrosanct relationships and institutions in our country suggests that more than just individual factors cause and support this type of criminal behavior.

Even in professional circles, strong emotional reactions are evoked by criminals, even when the crimes are non-sexual in nature. Criminologists Yochelson and Samenow (1986) wrote:

> We ... express our contempt for the criminal's whole way of life, saying that he represents a menace to us and our families; that we have no respect, liking, or compassion for a person who constitutes such a danger; and that he should be confined and if he remains unchanged, buried for life. (p. 118).

The authors didn't stop at that. They went on to say, "the criminal has to realize that he is rotten to the core" (p. 138). Yochelson and Samenow argue that the development of self-disgust is part of the offender's recovery. In fact, such self-disdain fuels many unhealthy compensating behaviors, some of which may include sex crimes. Carnes (1983, 1989, 1991) has claimed for more than a decade that a shame dynamic promotes addictive behavior, much like that seen in many sex offenders. Additional research has shown that sexual addiction is correlated with more than half of all sexual crimes (Blanchard, 1990). It can be argued from this premise that fueling offenders' self-disgust could actually escalate assaultive behavior. It is a disgust for one's sexually exploitive behavior that must be developed, not a disgust with one's complete self.

In his extraordinarily important book *Violence: Our Deadly Epidemic and Its Causes* (1996), James Gilligan argues that shame has become the primary and ultimate cause of all violence. "The purpose of violence," he wrote, "is to diminish the intensity of shame and replace it as far as possible with its opposite, pride, thus preventing the individual from being overwhelmed by the feeling of shame" (p. 111). If society, the courts, or therapists add shame to the violence equation, we can only expect even more violence.

Helping professionals often lament the fact that societal attitudes, both within and outside their ranks, profoundly influence the delivery of services to sexual criminals. After all, therapy operates in social and political arenas (Robitscher, 1980). Both justice and psychotherapy can be influenced by public attitudes of vengeance, retaliation, and a desire to punish. For example, the courts have followed widely disparate sentencing practices, seemingly in response to public pressure (Burkett & Bruni, 1993). Psychological evaluators frequently speak of the pressures imposed on them by prosecuting or defense attorneys who desire an evaluation that will support their case.

Finkelhor and Lewis (1987) described a dilemma that faces many helping professionals: On one hand, the public, media, and politicians clamor for harsh punishment of sexual offenders; on the other, treatment providers insist that punishing the perpetrators does little to protect the public. Many of us feel pressure from non-professionals who would prefer to dictate the style and conditions of treatment. When emotion rules, the fundamentals of democracy can fail. When we acquiesce to social or political pressure, the fundamentals of good counseling are all too frequently sacrificed.

In calling for castration legislation as a treatment/punishment response, Washington Senator Bob McCaslin dismissed arguments against cruel and unusual punishment by saying, "No one mentions cruel and unusual punishment of the citizens" ("Washington state senate," 1990, p. 2). The legislative impact of such measures on criminology and psychology may not only steer helping professionals away from humane counseling principles, it can also distract us from the guiding tenets of some of our country's greatest democratic and moral leaders.

Many years ago, Karl Menninger (1966) alerted us to the duplicitous ways in which the public linked justice and punishment. With great insight he called attention to the phenomena of distancing and objectification and showed how they precede punishment. Menninger also saw the desire to punish as a cloak for society's unhealthy desire for vengeance.

At the same time, Menninger (1966) acknowledged the needs for public safety, criminal penalties, and the swift implementation of consequences; he was never soft on crime. To the contrary, he strongly believed that penalties should be "greater and surer and quicker in coming" (p. 202). Poignantly, he argued:

> Being against punishment is not a sentimental conviction. It is a logical conclusion drawn from scientific experience. It is also a professional principle; we doctors try to relieve pain, not cause it. (p. 204).

Vengeance, Menninger (1966) contended, was like a two-edged sword: pain couldn't be relieved and crime couldn't be eliminated by stabbing one another. He further wrote:

> And just so long as the spirit of vengeance has the slightest vestige of respectability, so long as it pervades the public mind and infuses its evil upon the statute books of law, we will make no headway toward the control of crime. (p. 218).

Individual interventions alone can be of only limited value when it is understood that sex crimes are but one symptom of a violent American society. Clark (1970), Herman (1988), Strean and Freeman (1993), Gilligan (1996) and many more sociologists, criminologists, anthropologists, and psychologists have advanced similar ideas. Even as long ago as 1931, John L. Gillin, in *Taming the Criminal*, saw the foolishness of treating crime only as individual pathology. Gillin (1931) remarked, "How silly of us to think that we can prepare men for social life by reversing the ordinary process of socialization" (p. 137). By no means do I suggest that the individual perpetrator of sex crimes is without responsibility for his acts. He must assume personal ownership for his crime and experience stern consequences. Yet we must simultaneously give our attention to the cultural climate that propagates inhumanity.

Strean and Freeman (1993) refer to America as a "hate culture." They contend that the media's preoccupation with violence and murder reflects a culture that psychologically, if not legally, endorses such acts. As shown in the media's coverage of the death of serial killer Ted Bundy, our society feels every bit as murderous toward killers as the killers do toward their victims. Angry crowds cheered and celebrated the moment Bundy's death was announced and when the hearse carrying his body drove by. Events like this tap natural human feelings that showcase our disgust for violence. At the same time, they reveal our attraction to it. Publicly, many people abhor violence while privately they applaud it.

Will a violent response to violence eliminate violence? There is little evidence that it will. Should our goal be vengeance or should it be individual and societal change? Vengeance often motivates sexual crimes. Are we faced with a societal illness or an individual crime that needs eradication? The answer is both. If America is a violent society, and if we can conclude that vengeance is moral and valid, shall we argue that the entire national family deserves punishment? That seems doubtful. Begging the question may, however, encourage an etiological understanding of violence that leads us to individual and societal solutions that are less punitive and more restorative in nature. As violent crime escalates, we must escalate and broaden our response.

Despising criminals is an understandable reaction, but it is certainly not a solution. Despising violence, injustice, and exploitation is a more appropriate application of our angry energy. When society, aiming at justice, resorts to still more violence, injustice, and hatred, the criminal and this violent society have all of us in their grip. Inhumane punishment is symptomatic of an aggressive nation. Being criminal to criminals is itself criminal.

One guiding principle of sex offender treatment practice should be, to paraphrase Booker T. Washington, "Let no man pull you so low as to hate another." An appropriate societal response to sex offending requires an ability to interject logic and vision under extreme circumstances when emotion is inclined to rule. When a society begins to think in criminal ways, crime can only increase. When psychotherapists view sex offenders as subhuman, they may be persuaded to respond to them inhumanely. When criminologists suggest that condescending denigration has a place in rehabilitative programming, criminals will only harden their own beliefs toward people in general.

Yochelson and Samenow (1986), while almost certainly well-intentioned, wrote, "We inform the criminal that he may have a high IQ, but he has an equally high SQ, or stupidity quotient" (p. 135). A contrasting therapeutic approach has been taken for many years by humanistic psychologists who emphasized the pragmatic effectiveness of empathetic positive regard (Rogers, 1961b) and self-actualization principles (Maslow, 1962). Today, those same tenets of humanistic practice have been successfully adapted to sex offender treatment programs (Warren & Green, 1997). Respect and dignity are once again finding their rightful place in therapeutic circles.

While one camp of therapists reflects society's pessimism regarding the successful treatment of sex offenders, another camp maintains a more optimistic view of human nature. The latter group sets out in search of the light within every client — that innate human potential for goodness with which everyone is said to be born. Many critics find this posture naïve and dangerous.

Although the effectiveness of humanistic treatment approaches has never been convincingly proven, some data suggest a level of success. One survey of sex offender treatment providers (Plyer, Woolley, & Anderson, 1990) showed that only 13.8% of community-based and 11.2% of institutional treatment providers reported that Rogerian or other humanistic approaches were not successful. Of nine modalities reviewed, the third-most-preferred treatment approach of community programs was humanistic, reflecting some belief in the efficacy of this approach. Outcome and recidivism studies, of course, remain problematic.

Unlike outpatient clinics, correctional facilities that offer sex-offender programming cannot always be expected to produce positive therapeutic outcomes, especially in prison environments that are notoriously hostile to inmates serving sentences for the sexual exploitation of children (Murphy & Dison, 1990). We can expect the penitentiary climate to be conducive to openness, self-examination, and growth only in rare instances.

Firm consequences and incarceration are frequently necessary to control sexual offending behavior. A humane prison environment, however, is an absolute necessity for the healing of sexually exploitive men, while a punitive setting serves only to perpetuate the violence of offenders who are sentenced to them (Gilligan, 1996).

Cultural Healing

This book challenges the reader to examine his/her attitudes toward sex criminals. It does not suggest tolerance for crime. It does, however, challenge everyone to consider the proposition that hatred and vengeance — no matter who the target — is the problem, not the solution for which we search. To eliminate violence from American life, we must confront the attitudes that exacerbate crime and support state-sanctioned crime. As Clarence Darrow (quoted in Larson & Micheels-Cyrus, p. 233) pointedly said, "If the State wishes that its citizens respect human life, then the State should stop killing." Analogously, if society desires to end sexual violence, it must rise above its desire to retaliate violently.

Dr. Fred Berlin of Johns Hopkins University has worked with sex offenders for many years. Instead of becoming calloused and cynical by the experience, he has developed a forbearing stance toward all of humanity — sex offenders included. In an article on sexual crimes (Kraxiec, 1990), Berlin made clear his values:

> We have to ask ourselves what values we want to instill in our own children. Revenge? I've seen children being taught to hate, and that just adds to the scarring. I want my children to value compassion, understanding, forgiveness, and mercy. (p. 51).

It is easy to state one's opposition to sex crimes. It is easy, as well, to assert that the answers to this epidemic are simple and swift. It may be comfortable to stand virtuously apart from society and point an accusing and indignant finger elsewhere. Yet, as Erich Fromm (1987) was quoted as saying, "There is perhaps no phenomenon which conveys so much destructive feeling as moral indignation, which permits envy or hate to be acted out under the guise of virtue" (p. 147).

It has been said that we punish only because we do not know what else to do (Bazelon, 1961). As knowledge has advanced, sex criminals who were once deemed to be untreatable are now being found suitable for our best attempts at rehabilitation. Still, a broader question remains. Can America be rehabilitated? Criminologists, anthropologists, and psychologists are now offering helpful guidance on individual lifestyle changes that collectively can result in a healthful societal evolution.

> *Non-violence is the answer to the crucial political and moral questions of our time; the need for man to overcome oppression and violence without resorting to oppression and violence. Man must evolve for all human conflict a method which rejects revenge, aggression and retaliation.*
>
> — Martin Luther King, Jr.
> (Quoted in Larson & Micheels-Cyrus, 1987, p. 168)

CHAPTER 2

The Normality of Sexual Offenders

An individual who engages in these deviant behaviors may be automatically assumed to be mentally disordered.

— Seymour Halleck (1967, p. 77)

The exploiter is the ordinary person, perhaps a kind and caring person in some ways, and it is this which needs to be taken on.

— Janice Russell (1993, p. 54)

E ARLIER I MENTIONED that most people are more comfortable viewing sexual assaultiveness as individual pathology rather than as a symptom of a dysfunctional society. Many experts now believe that the acceptance of sexual aggression is part and parcel of American male psychology. Sex crimes are a reflection of normal male values, publicly denied by most men, yet acted on with alarming frequency. Speaking of sex offenders, psychiatrist Judith Herman warns, "The most striking characteristic from a diagnostic standpoint, is their apparent normality" (1988, p. 702). What isn't normal in many of the men arrested for sex offenses is their intense and often addictive attachment to sex, especially sexual urges and fantasies involving children. However, the denial of individual sexual aggression, the media's unintended promotion of this behavior, and the many cultural supports for sexual aggression sustain a climate conducive to sexual exploitation (Freeman-Longo & Blanchard, 1998). Sexual violence is as American as apple pie; it is a stark and painful acknowledgment of our cultural condition.

There are certainly many offenders who fit the tidy diagnostic categories covered by the personality disorders listed in the *l Manual of Mental Disorders, 4th Edition* Association, 1994). These men are often *tic, dependent, avoidant,* and so on. Yet most traits or belief systems that separate them hen. Consequently, psychological predictors of assaultive behavior are very difficult to pinpoint. "The great majority of convicted offenders do not suffer from psychiatric conditions (psychotic disorders or severe mental retardation) that might be invoked to diminish criminal responsibility," according to Herman (1988, p. 699).

A. Nicholas Groth (1983), an expert on sexual aggression, views rapists and child molesters as individuals who are suffering more from problems of emotional immaturity than emotional disturbance. He said, "When we are talking about sexual assault, we are talking about a behavior that anyone could exhibit ..." (p. 37).

UCLA researcher Neil Malamuth (1985) revealed an alarming finding: 60% of American men would force a woman to commit sexual acts against her will if assured that they would not be caught. When Malamuth changed a questionnaire phrase from "commit sexual acts" to the loaded term "rape," about 20% of American men still said they would commit such an act against a woman as long as the crime would not be discovered.

A significant portion of the male population not only endorses rape-supportive attitudes and finds the fantasy of rape acceptable, but also becomes sexually aroused by depictions of rape (Herman, 1988). Many women also admit being turned on by fantasies of being raped. These observations do not, however, automatically suggest that most men will rape or that women want to be raped. The difference between normality and criminality is often that ability to clearly separate fantasy from reality or to incorporate values that limit one's behavior.

The results of a random sample telephone survey found that up to 17% of the male population admitted having molested a child (Finkelhor & Lewis, 1988, p. 66). The methodology used guaranteed the respondent's anonymity. If that many men admitted to sexual contact with children, might the actual prevalence be even higher, assuming some perpetrators may have been in denial? Could child molestation be a relatively "normal" American male experience too? Does child sexual abuse reflect as much on our culture as on the individuals who perpetrate such crimes? Stephen Rossetti's words in *Slayer of the Soul* offer a chilling rejoinder: "The existence of pedophilia and ephebephilia might be seen as a symptom of an underlying disorder within our entire society" (1990, p. 187).

"Well-adjusted" Americans carry within them some of the same types of hatred, sexual fantasies, and violent potential that is uncovered in convicted sexual abusers (Gruen, 1992). While working hard to appear "proper," most people fail to detect their own potentially destructive dark sides. When that disowned and neglected part surfaces and a sexual crime is committed, almost everyone stands back in disbelief, saying, "It can't be so." Our collective denial is very apparent. Yet, when an individual is convicted o f a sex crime, we are quick to attack any signs of denial in him.

Despite convincing evidence that sexual offenders do not stand out as strikingly abnormal, a significant number — perhaps a minority — engage in aberrant sex acts known as paraphilias. Paraphilias fall outside the normally accepted range of sexual behavior. They are a group of disorders in which sexual excitement is contingent on the presence of an unusual or bizarre fantasy or behavior. Among the identified paraphilias are exhibitionism, voyeurism, pedophilia, obscene phone calling, and sexual sadism. While an average man may entertain unusual fantasies, the individual addicted to one or more paraphilias has lost the ability to manage his fantasy life: he repeatedly acts out the desired behavior. Many times it is this loss of control, primarily in this one area of his life, that separates him from most men. Yet when these men are observed in the community, the vast majority of their interpersonal relationships appear to be quite normal.

Psychiatrist and author Richard Gardner stirred controversy when he wrote, "...there is a bit of pedophilia in every one of us."

(1991, p. 118). His experience is that many people, upon hearing of child sexual abuse, gratify a pedophilic impulse that usually doesn't reach conscious awareness. Gardner goes so far as to assert that many individuals, through projection, attribute to others the very impulses with which they are struggling. Briere and Runtz (1989) and Smiljanich (1992) researched the prevalence of sexual arousal to children in groups of nonclinical, nonincarcerated males. As many as 21% of the respondents described a sexual attraction to at least some small children. These findings do not support Gardner's contentions to the extent that he claims. Yet whichever number is more accurate — 100% (Gardner's "every one") or 21% — pedophilic urges are frighteningly common in our culture. As Briere (1992) asserts: "The presence of so many pedophilic-like individuals in relatively high-functioning, 'normal' samples supports the notion that the sexualization of children is at least partially a social phenomenon" (p. 94).

While Yochelson and Samenow are reported by Hylton to have referred to criminals as a "different breed" (1981, p. 12), they actually share more commonalities than differences with most of us. Consequently, all men must be open to examining their own criminal potential and the ways they may perpetuate the notion that sex criminals are dramatically different from the norm. What frequently separates many criminals from non-criminals is that criminals are caught, while others are not.

Sexually Exploitive Helping Professionals

The normality of sex offending has become even more apparent with the recent revelations regarding helping professionals who rape, exploit, and molest. Seemingly normal and trustworthy individuals such as clerics, psychologists, psychiatrists, counselors, social workers, physicians, teachers, police, and attorneys are regularly being convicted of sex crimes against the clientele they are responsible for helping. So unwilling are these professional groups to self-examine honestly that a separate set of nomenclature is used to describe their sexual exploitation. Instead of calling this abuse of power a sex offense — or even a paraphilia — helping professionals and even some of their respective licensing boards prefer to describe this assaultiveness as "affairs," "trysts," or simply "sexual impairment" (Irons, 1993). Most recently, the terms "professional sexual misconduct" and "sexual behavior problems" have become more popular.

Churches and professional associations have gone to great lengths to protect their images before their parishioners and clients. The Roman Catholic Church (and most certainly other faiths) has used cash payments, much like hush money, to silence victims and to avoid publicity (Burkett & Bruni, 1992). Organizations like the American Psychiatric Association have been accused of cover-ups that further exploited assault victims ("My Doctor, My Lover," Storring, 1991). In 1993, The National Association of Social Workers sponsored licensing legislation in Wyoming (HB169) that would allow counselors to sexually exploit clients three times before the act became a felony. Many have concluded that the helping professions are not yet ready to face what has for years been a frequent problem in their ranks — the sexual exploitation of parishioners and patients. When even the "helpers" exploit, it is exceedingly difficult to regard sex offending as a phenomenon found only among a few perverted and abnormal people.

Beginning in 1984, a national trend toward criminalizing this type of professional misconduct has reached at least eight states which have enacted legislation. No longer can we excuse these acts as minor ethical lapses. No longer can they be minimized by the very professions who have the responsibility for treating this type of misconduct in others. The number of lawsuits against mental health professionals engaging in "sexual misconduct" with their clients has increased over the past few years.

Unless the helping professions honestly address sex offending within their own ranks, what safe haven remains for victims who desire spiritual and psychological counseling? Will victims conclude that because everyone seems to be doing it, sex offending should be regarded as a normal hazard of living in this culture — something they must learn to accept?

Sociocultural Factors

Sociocultural explanations for sex crimes are supported by the work of anthropologist Peggy Reeves Sanday. It may come as a surprise to an ethnocentric culture like ours that sexual assaultiveness is not a world-wide phenomenon. In fact, Sanday contends, there are rape-free cultures. Their existence further advances the theory that sex crimes are generated not only by individual pathology or biological forces, but by the very culture in which a person lives.

Sanday (1981) cited several features characteristic of rape-free cultures:

- Women are treated with great respect.
- Women are viewed as influential members of their community.
- Women contribute equally with men.
- Women have similar labor roles as men.
- Women are economically independent.
- Women experience no limits on their mobility (the places they can frequent).

In comparison, rape-prone societies, such as that of the United States, share the following characteristics:

- There is worship of a male creator/deity.
- Women are the primary nurturers of children, while men primarily assume the role of disciplinarian.
- Husbands are positioned as the head of the household. They provide for the family, protect them, and control them.
- Boys are taught to be tough and aggressive.
- Competition is valued as a way to demonstrate superiority and dominance.

- Competition provides men with a means by which they can establish their value and esteem.
- Warfare is glorified.

It is, as former U.S. Attorney General Ramsey Clark wrote, "America's national character and condition ... [that] creates capabilities of crime" (1970, p. 37). Of course, this insight is not intended to absolve convicted sex offenders of their crimes. Personal accountability and humane consequences must always be a part of the solution to crime.

Most facilitators of sexual offenders' groups say that the therapeutic issues addressed in treatment also are of use in their own personal lives. For instance: power, dominance, competition, control, anger, low self-esteem, spiritual emptiness, objectification of women and children, depression, loneliness, rape fantasies, and so on are matters with which most American men regularly grapple.

Strean and Freeman (1993) draw a very powerful conclusion in their book *Our Wish to Kill*. They contend that most Americans are similar to violent criminals, including rapists and murderers. In their words, "It is far easier to verbally attack the rapist and murder the killer, than to face our inner wishes to rape and murder" (p. 83). They believe that only when we Americans can accept this dark side of ourselves can we begin to develop a safer society in which to live. When this nation begins to understand its own violent impulses, the door will open to a greater understanding of sex offenders. At the same time, our impulses toward retaliation will diminish when personal understanding increases. With understanding, they argue, comes the awareness that, "There, but for the grace of God, go I."

Cultural Solutions

As long as we have a dichotomous mindset that neatly pigeonholes people into categories of "good guys" and "bad guys," no answers to the problem of sexual assaultiveness will be forthcoming. Instead, we must view sexual exploitation on a continuum on which all people are located, each person contributing in some way — from subtle to blatant — to the perpetuation of sexual aggression. When Americans can more honestly identify the prevalence of sexually aggressive urges in its population, and reduce the cultural supports for them, we will have made a significant stride toward reducing sex offenses. Similarly, when we educate our children to understand that people do harmful things not just because they are "bad" but many times because they are wounded or needy, then they can be prepared to examine their own feelings and behaviors later in life when troubling urges surface.

After all, the criminal is like ourselves, is he not?

— Marcel Courtemanche (1982, p. 25)

CHAPTER 3

The Mechanization of Treatment

Research exploring the use of a variety of physiological monitors, including pupilography, penile temperature changes, measurement of penile length changes (in addition to circumference changes), computerized electroencephalographic responses, and even positron emission tomography of the central nervous system is brisk and, combined with plethysmographic data, promises more comprehensive and hopefully valid barometers of sexual response in the future.

— Barry Maletzky (1991, p. 33)

When technique is made paramount, everything is lost because the very essence of the authentic relationship is that one does not manipulate but turns toward another with one's whole being.

— Irving Yalom (1980, p. 410)

BEFORE ALL ELSE, psychotherapy is a human relationship, a highly personal encounter between two people embarking on a mutual journey toward change. As a part of a safe relationship, clients can risk self-examination of painful truths and accept responsibility for their shortcomings. From the foundation of a healthy relationship, the client begins what is frequently a reparative process that can heal prior traumatic relationships and give birth to new ways of interacting with his peers. As Aponte and Winter (1987) wrote, "... the vehicle for therapeutic change is a social relationship" (p. 85). It is the process of inter-personal relating that heals more effectively than the accomplishment of any therapeutic tasks or goals. There is no data to suggest that humans convicted of sex crimes are an exception to this counseling rule.

Yet psychotherapy operates within the sphere of influence of politics and social norms, and counselors often are persuaded to distance themselves emotionally from the sex offenders they are called to treat. Societal pressures can work against developing the "compassionate responsiveness" that Perlman (1979, p. 31) saw as essential to change. Some therapists act out society's animosities (or their own) toward sex offenders by being distant, excessively judgmental, condescending, or punitive. But what is needed is a caring, firm, and respectful confrontation, and it can be effectively accomplished without emotionally battering the offender. Certainly, asking a counselor to show care toward someone who is responsible for a disgusting crime creates a difficult and demanding expectation. And, while it is important that we afford this man the equivalent respect given other clients, we have the right to expect him to fulfill his obligation to practice the same with regard to us.

When the fundamentals of relationship-building are not applied to sex offenders, little movement or growth will take place in counseling. Seeing their lack of progress, the helping professional frequently (and erroneously) concludes that sex offenders have an innately poor prognosis with little, if any, chance for restoration. This is a classic example of self-fulfilling prophecy.

Not everyone shares an optimistic viewpoint about the efficacy of therapeutic interventions with sex offenders. One isolated research study reported in the *Minneapolis Star Tribune* ("Incest offenders," 1991) claimed incarcerated sex offenders recovered at higher rates and were less inclined to reoffend if no counseling was provided. A group of offenders who were part of a therapeutic intervention demonstrated a rate of recidivism 40% higher than untreated men. Based on this study one might hastily conclude that psychotherapy has no place in the dangerous world of sex offending. Strong arguments can be made, however, that the success observed by many other treatment facilities is more than a self-serving observation. And, of course, efficacy and outcome always depend on the quality of the treatment. Sex offenders can make great strides, especially when certain factors are in place:

- Comprehensive treatment is provided that is not reliant on a single therapeutic modality but includes features from many.
- Comprehensive differential diagnostic assessments are performed.
- Appropriate referrals are made from the assessments that take into consideration the uniqueness of each offender and the treatment providers best suited to him.
- Overlapping addictions, particularly sexual and chemical addictions, are simultaneously treated.
- Treatment providers relate to each offender on a humanistic basis, not just from a sterile medical model or a punitive law enforcement approach.

Tools of the Trade

While I suggest more emphasis on the personal relationship in treating sex offenders, I do not suggest that anyone dismiss the usefulness of mechanistic techniques. Instrumentation clearly has its place in the overall treatment of sex offenders. Yet, the trend toward developing and using hardware, in and of itself, will not always guarantee long-term changes in men who are themselves inclined to depersonalize their victims. A closer examination of this trend also shows how the potentially disrespectful features of many mechanical treatment techniques, when improperly used, can negatively affect the offender's self-esteem, contrary to the rehabilitative task of raising the offender's self-esteem.

One commonly cited technique is *olfactory aversion therapy*. Noxious odors are paired with deviant sexual imagery in order to extinguish aberrant arousal patterns. Both on a self-administered basis and in a professionally monitored clinical setting, the sex offender receives a blast of a noxious odor in his nasal cavity whenever he catches himself responding with arousal to deviant fantasies. Among the commonly used odors are ammonia, valeric acid, and rotting tissue.

Phallometry is used to monitor erection response associated with sexual arousal. While sexual crimes involve genitalia, and while a sex offender's sexual fantasies must be addressed, the clinician must look deeper for the etiological origins of assaultive patterns and not just measure and treat their symptoms. Too frequently, phallometry is used prematurely prior to — or even as a complete substitute for — a detailed clinical interview. Clinical interviews build client rapport and the client/professional relationship.

Masturbatory satiation is another genitally focused technique. Also referred to as *orgasmic reconditioning*, sexual offenders are asked to masturbate to "healthy" sexual fantasies while recording their thoughts into a tape-recorder. Then, upon reaching orgasm, the offender is encouraged to immediately begin masturbating again, this time to one of his deviant sexual fantasies. It is hoped that he will have little pleasure during the second masturbatory experience and that, too, will be recorded on tape. His therapist then reviews the tapes to monitor client progress.

This technique obviously conflicts with *celibacy contracting*, a common component in the treatment of the sexually addicted sex offender. It can also conflict with the client's religious beliefs. Caution should always be used when using techniques that intrude on the client's personal space, privacy, or acceptable belief system. A person addicted to sex does not benefit from practicing new kinds of sex in the acute stages of recovery. Much like an alcoholic, he will need a detoxifying period in which he "dries out" and discovers what emotions were being suppressed by regularly using mood-altering experiences that involved sex and/or violence.

Electric shock (another type of aversion therapy, not to be confused with electroconvulsive therapy) is used by a few technicians. Pairing pain with deviant sexual fantasies is intended to reduce aberrant thoughts — at least over the short term. Present data suggest that electric shock is not effective in reducing deviant arousal, nor is it widely used among sex offender treatment programs in America (Knopp, Freeman-Longo, & Stevenson, 1992). While Maletzky

(1991) points out that some sexual offenders are wrong to characterize this treatment approach as "barbarism, torture and medical experimentation" (p. 114), perhaps it is the offenders who can best speak to their own reality.

Chemotherapy has been shown to be an effective method of curbing sexual arousal. Medroxyprogesterone acetate, or Depo-Provera, when properly administered, is still thought to have a wide range of medical side effects. With the ease of writing a prescription, the psychiatrist can temporarily lower serum testosterone levels and observe results without having to invest time or effort in counseling. An erroneous assumption is that once the sexual drive is in check, little else needs to be done in the restorative process. Always, personal counseling and a comprehensive treatment approach must accompany this form of treatment. There are many factors beyond sexual arousal that give rise to assaultiveness and must be simultaneously treated.

Currently, politicians in some states are entering into the therapeutic and medical arenas by passing legislation that mandates all convicted sex offenders be "chemically castrated." In essence, lay people are prescribing drugs to treat sex offenders with no regard for the ethical and health consequences of their acts. Like many people in our own field, politicians are looking for quick and effective techniques that can eradicate sexual abuse.

Polygraph examinations are gaining popularity as a treatment technique used with both adult and juvenile sex offenders. Some programs now use polygraphy to extract "the truth" from sex offender clients regarding the exact nature of their sexual assaultiveness. The abuse of technology, when it is used, is always a potential problem. In some programs, clients are advised that polygraph results are definitive and will be potentially damning in adjudicating their case. The client is then told he will soon be transported to a polygraph examiner, where the truth will come out. He is told to "get honest" and "fess up" before the exam if he is to expect any kind of lenient treatment. In these extreme cases, the clinician's dishonesty and the reliance on instrumentation becomes a dangerous combination.

When this type of approach is used, the therapeutic relationship can be very adversely affected.

Many other techniques and instruments are used with sex offenders, frequently as a substitute for good counseling skills. These techniques should be regarded only as potentially helpful adjuncts to the counseling relationship, rather than as substitutes. While their long-term usefulness and their humane qualities are under scrutiny by many researchers and practitioners in the field, a growing number of caring clinicians are integrating these techniques into comprehensive and humanistically oriented treatment programs.

Technique vs. Relationship

The therapist, using his/her self, is the primary "tool" for initiating change in offenders. "The dynamics of therapy...," as Whitaker and Malone argued, "...are in the person of the therapist" (1953, p. 62). The quality of the therapist-patient relationship is equally important, if not more so, than any technique or instrument in restoring sex offenders to safe and healthy relationships within society. Of course, a warm counseling persona alone, without technical competence and an authoritative demeanor, can be a dangerous thing.

A seasoned offender will sense when a naïve clinician's only tool is the relationship, and he may attempt to charm his way through therapy: "Ya know, I've been to several therapists over the past two years and never have I worked with anyone with your knowledge and compassion. I'm looking forward to therapy sensing that we will get along very well." The tacit message amidst this offender's false praise was actually a poorly disguised bribe: if the therapist would skip unpleasant confrontations the offender would assure the therapist of continued adulation. An effective therapeutic response might have been: "I attempt to treat all my patients the same — with warmth, dignity, and firmness. At times I will respectfully confront you and then your opinion of me might change somewhat. As you probably know, some tests and conflicts are unnatural in any relationship. With me, I believe you will find a firm honesty that will push you at times, but always in a healthy direction. I'll expect your honesty in return."

Virginia Satir always asserted that it was the personal development of the therapist, including the skills of using one's personality and self to their fullest, that begins the client change process. In her direct fashion Satir once said:

> In my mind, learning to be a therapist is not like learning to be a plumber. Plumbers can usually settle for techniques. Therapists need to do more. You don't have to love a pipe to fix it. (Satir & Baldwin, 1983, p. 227).

This viewpoint implies that to the extent the helping professional is self-aware, fully integrated, and caring, s/he will bring about a healing process in the offenders with whom s/he works.

Collier (1987) wrote,

> It seems transparently clear to me that the most important choice for our clients is not which technique will help them best (though this too is important), but which therapist will offer the widest and most flexible response as an individual to the clients as individuals. (p. 59).

A responsible therapist will not only model an adaptable personhood, but will manifest respect and care for the offender. It is a mature and respectful way of relating that contributes to a healthy personality. The first step in developing this type of respect and care toward an individual whose acts we find reprehensible is to be willing to try to understand the person. Not to *immediately* understand him/her, but to initially *try* to understand him/her. While our own prejudices may hamper our attempts at understanding, it is the willingness to try that counts. At the same time, one must never convey the message that understanding somehow excuses offending behavior. A therapeutic clarification may sound like this: "I'm going to do my best to understand your traumatic life history and how it contributed to your assault pattern. With those insights I believe you will be able to make more responsible choices in the days ahead."

Sex offenders are rarely confused by therapists who are firm, moralize about crime and, at the same time, show respect and concern for their clients. Remember, a caring demeanor doesn't have to reflect weakness. Most criminals I have known don't respect weakness. Caring is about strength that arises from a secure individual who advocates for developing a client's good side no matter the societal pressure s/he feels. If the clinician is going to teach the client empathy, s/he must model empathy. Modeling empathy requires that you show care, concern, and respect for all humans within treatment sessions and outside them.

When moralizing, we are not shaming or judging the client. We are, however, passing on society's values regarding offending behavior. And in doing so, we appeal to the offender's core values, those that are held close to his heart — values that he may have suspended during the assaults. Our role is to resurrect a sense of moral obligation to the community, to help the offender rediscover and apply the moral rules they already, as social beings, possess to some degree (Doherty, 1995).

"Therapy is a personal relationship operating within the parameters of a professional structure" wrote Aponte and Winter (1987, p. 93). If you are visibly personable to your colleagues and relate very differently to an offender, he is likely to conclude that duplicity is acceptable. Your true personality, visible at all times, will help establish a meaningful therapeutic connection.

If you find yourself needing to have the upper hand at all times with the offender, you have probably joined him in a power struggle. If you display concern and respect in the client/therapist relationship, power differentials often equalize. This is acceptable as long as the therapist maintains a professional role and isn't seen as simply a friend. One doesn't have to command power over another to bring about change. Power comes with the law and its swift enforcement of consequences. The therapist can be allied with the law and at the same time with offender clients without any confusion in roles.

Yalom (1980) cautions clinicians that it is very easy to assume their clients are responding to some specific technique, when actually the deciding variable has everything to do with the therapist's humanness. We do like our gimmicks, techniques, and instruments, but nothing is so valuable as an available sense of self that nonadversarially reaches out to help others. Perhaps what really happens is that the gimmick turns the clinician's key, opening the door to ourselves and enabling us to make ourselves available to the client rather than changing the client.

Where the spirit does not work with the hand there is no art.

— Leonardo Da Vinci (Quoted in Andrews, 1991, p. 187)

CHAPTER 4

Who Owns Resistance?

Resistance is an operational concept; it is nothing new that is created by the analysis; the analytic situation only becomes the arena for these forces of resistance to show themselves.

— Ralph Greenson (1987, p. 135)

Just as the rigid authoritarian parent virtually creates a rebellious attitude in the child, the technique-dominated analyst creates a great deal of resentment in the patient.

— Reuben Fine (1985, pp.14-15)

ONE ARGUMENT GOES: "Some of the most resistant clients I have ever worked with are sex offenders." Nearly all clinicians who have worked with this client population have, at one time or another, felt that way or heard similar comments. It is difficult to be in a helping relationship when a client appears to resist one's every effort.

Resistance, by definition, is any force that works against the counseling process. Generally, this translates to noncompliance (either active or passive) with the therapist's agenda. When a sex offender isn't following the therapist's plan in accordance with a pre-ordained schedule, it is often interpreted by the clinician as a personal affront. Countertransference (an alternate term for therapist resistance) soon develops. Therapy quickly becomes an "us vs. them" encounter, a test of wills, a power struggle.

I often say in my lectures, "There is no such thing as a resistant client, only therapists who don't know how to connect." Occasionally, I temper this provocative remark with a qualifier, suggesting that by exaggeration my point is made: resistance can result from not having developed strong relationship-building skills.

Sometimes, offender resistance is simply an adaptive mechanism used to cope with an unresponsive or insensitive therapist. In essence, we often unintentionally help the offender dig his way into an unyielding position of angry recalcitrance.

Lazarus and Fay (1982) saw resistance as nothing more than the defense mechanism of rationalization used by therapists who could not accept responsibility for their treatment failures, which stem from an inability to connect. When, on the other hand, the therapist becomes open to the meaning behind an offender's style of non-cooperation, opportunities for responsive communication unfold, understanding may increase, and growth may take place.

There are some clients who simply do not want to be a part of any treatment effort. They will sabotage treatment, set themselves up to fail, and refuse to comply with the therapeutic process. In some cases, however, resistance may have little or nothing to do with "criminal personalities," deep-seated characterological issues, or personality disorders. In the case of an inexperienced, poorly trained, or unskilled clinician, the client's resistance may represent factors that say more about the quality of the therapist's intervention or counseling style than the offender's intentions. For example:

- Resistance may arise from fear, a feeling of being unsafe.
- Resistance may signal that the therapist is moving too fast in the counseling process.
- Resistance may arise when the offender does not feel reinforced for the positive efforts he has shown.
- Resistance may arise from feeling misunderstood.
- Resistance may be in response to the therapist's inflexibility or judgmentalness.
- Resistance may be a response to being labeled as mentally disordered.
- Resistance may arise in response to the use of threats or coercion that were intended to elicit change.
- Resistance may spring from distrust of the therapist's poorly communicated motives and goals.

- Resistance and bitterness may be in response to the fees being charged.

Additionally,
- The therapist may be boring.
- The therapist may be approaching the offender in a cold, impersonal, or mechanical way.
- The therapist may not be in touch with his own power and control needs, which he is acting out on the offender.

And,
- The offender may feel he has been defined by his aggressive acts only.
- The offender may feel apprehension about getting too close to the therapist.
- The offender may indirectly be telling the therapist how much he does not appreciate the way he is being treated.
- The offender may not feel accepted at any level by persons in the legal or therapeutic system.

To understand resistance, therapists must first look inward. Usually, it is necessary to reframe for ourselves the offender's behavior if we are to stay emotionally disentangled. It is always best to see resistance not as a personal attack, but as a learning opportunity that can teach us how to be more effective as clinicians. It is when the therapist feels attacked — especially by someone s/he does not respect — that s/he overlooks the insights all around her/him. Once s/he feels attacked, a therapist may counterattack by blaming the client or assigning a pejorative label (e.g., antisocial, deviant, resistant, etc.). Kottler (1992) agreed when he wrote, "When therapists encounter something they do not like or cannot understand, the first thing they do is label it" (p. 127). Playfully, some therapists refer to this professional propensity as a disease called "hardening of the categories." When difficulties arise, almost always the problem is assumed to lie outside ourselves and within the client. If the offender can be labeled, then implicitly, the responsibility must lie exclusively with him.

Greenson's (1987) chapter on "Resistance Analysis" in *Techniques of Working with Resistance* (Milman & Goldman, 1987, pp. 133-166), explains that it is common for therapists to create resistance by demanding certain things from their clients or acting in such ways that the most reasonable response is to resist the relationship. According to deShazer (1984) resistance is a figment of our imagination. Client non-cooperation, he argued, is not about resistance as much as it is the client's awkward attempts to teach therapists how to be more helpful, respectful, or responsive. Kottler (1992) has responded to the work of deShazer, saying, "Every client has a unique way of communicating and cooperating in therapy; it is our job to discover what that way is and to make the best use of it" (p. 183). Again, one is reminded of the importance of polishing and using good diagnostic skills, developing the attitude of concerned detachment, and attempting to connect by careful understanding. A useful rule of thumb is: as understanding increases, resistance diminishes. Put into action, concerned detachment matched with understanding may be conveyed to the offender in this fashion: "I sense that something is getting in the way of our working relationship. This will happen from time to time. Together we can get past these temporary obstacles. If you can help me better understand your discomfort I can help you more. Let's look at our relationship for a moment."

If the therapist has made a valiant effort to understand the dynamics of resistance (including participation in professional and/or peer supervision) and is still met with obstructionism, a determination can then be made regarding the client's prognosis. When we have done our best to examine and reexamine resistance and we still find the offender uncooperative, it probably suggests that he carries a poor prognosis for recovery and represents a serious continuing threat to society. Under those circumstances, and should an appropriate referral to another therapist prove unsuccessful (since even the best therapist and the most willing client may simply not be a good match), further legal consequences may be the only effective recourse — the only effective way to communicate with the offender.

Countertransference Triggers

How do these men get to us? Or as one group facilitator asked, "What is it about that guy that brings out all the worst in me?" It may be that therapists are just as emotionally vulnerable as many of the people they work with. Helpers have wounds that can easily be inflamed. When a therapist gets emotionally "hooked" by a sex offender, a number of factors may explain the situation:

- The therapist may have lost (or never developed) the ability to pull back and observe the client interaction. An anthropologist's viewpoint is often helpful.
- The sex offender may have violated the therapist's fundamental values of decency, sensitivity, and fairness.
- The offender may have triggered unresolved sexual, physical, or emotional abuse issues in the therapist's past.
- The offender may remind the therapist of an individual about whom s/he still carries some unresolved emotional baggage.
- Therapy may feel like a one-sided affair — all give and no take. Resentment is never far behind this feeling.
- The therapist may find him/herself relating in an unnatural manner in response to political, societal, or legal pressures.
- The therapist may have high expectations of the offender that are not being met.

On the other hand, the therapist's positive regard for the offender may also be heightened by the type of connected relationship being recommended in this book. Resulting countertransference reactions offer some of the best clues available to understand the offender's social skills deficits. From this perspective, countertransference can be seen as a therapeutic aid rather than a shortcoming.

Difficult People

Difficult people can be hostile, manipulative, abrasive, or avoidant. Among their ranks are many fearful and insecure people, including sex offenders — and many helping professionals. If the therapist responds solely to what the difficult person is saying, rather than to his communication style, s/he will fail to understand that individual's psychology. When a sex offender screams obscenities in the therapist's face and threatens bodily harm, his method of communication is more revealing than his words. The sex offender's fear may be masked by an intimidating bravado. How difficult it is to recognize this fact when the most urgent needs seem to be self-protection and limit-setting! Later reflection, accompanied by a fair level of depersonalization, may help to unearth the secret messages of his communication style.

Angry people are secretly fearful people — fearful of being embarrassed, put-down, criticized, or losing control. Their rage is an adaptive effort to return a semblance of control or homeostasis to a life that is spinning out of control. Angry resistance can best be understood as the desperate attempt of a cornered individual to assuage his feelings of fearfulness and powerlessness.

Manipulation is a less emotional, more cerebral method of acquiring control over people and situations. Some offenders use a carefully calculated style of communication that is designed to divert conversations, confuse, or convince counselors to see things their way. Their communication does not address the main issue. Often they will use compliments and praise as a way to control the therapist. When a therapist uses covert attempts to control, persuade, or change the offender, it should not be surprising to find that the client quickly responds in kind, and nothing meaningful is accomplished.

Abrasiveness, of the Don Rickles variety, is always difficult to cope with. When a sex offender keeps on coming with his cynical and vitriolic tongue, it is not that he truly feels as superior and righteous as he proclaims. Generally, he feels snubbed and impotent in human interactions. He craves intimacy but fears closeness. Rather than express his vulnerabilities and risk a painful rejection, this offender projects a false image of invulnerability. Unfortunately, his communication style causes him further social alienation. What the therapist can offer this man is a patient willingness to look beyond the caustic verbiage and to persist in discovering the core goodness hidden within.

Avoidant communicators are quietly frustrating, as their "all is well" comments belie their often tragic inner existence. When an offender uses a protective defense of emotional insulation, therapists often mistakenly assume their client's silence is about obstinance. Avoidant offenders tend to somaticize problems and communicate their pain in indirect ways. As with other difficult communicators, fear is usually the root of this maladaptive style. Commonly, one sees this type of communication from child molesters. Asking such offenders to risk major change early in therapy is to invite resistance. We must move slowly with them to avoid their resistance to the therapy process.

Resistance as an Aid to Understanding

In many instances, an offender's resistance is his unconscious way of teaching the therapist how to get through to him. It isn't always a sign of noncooperation or lack of motivation. Encoded in resistant behavior are many tips on how one can best reach these men. Therapist countertransference can also provide helpful information on how to relate differently, and therefore more effectively, with sex offenders. Countertransference can also direct the therapist to his/her own inner wounds that need attention.

Not only can we learn more about the sex offender by his difficult communication style, we may also learn some things about ourselves and be afforded an opportunity for personal growth. Before

47

us is an opportunity to hone our skills of detachment and flexibility. With some resistant offenders we may repeatedly insist that more "clout" is required; that a "hammer over his head" is needed to enlist cooperation. But after enough experience with sex offenders, most clinicians agree that a carrot is better than a stick.

Resistance and countertransference are not inherently bad. They are simply momentary obstacles to effective communication. Once understood, they become our allies. Make good use of them.

Into the looking-glass the dog goes running. Seeing his own reflection, he dies barking.

— Kabir (Quoted in Andrews, 1991, p. 197)

CHAPTER 5

A Restorative Approach

To rehabilitate is to restore to a former constructive capacity or condition. There is nothing to which to rehabilitate a criminal.

— Stanton Samenow (1984, p. 203)

If I can get through to a person, even those whose behavior has a lot of destructive elements, I believe he or she would want to do the right thing.

— Carl Rogers (quoted in Baldwin & Satir, 1987, p. 50)

T O RESTORE, AS DEFINED in *Webster's New Dictionary and Thesaurus* (1990), means "to bring, put, or give back; to reestablish; to reinstate; to repair; to cure." For sex offenders there is no cure; there is only the hope of better self-control and behavior management (Knopp, 1984). Yet many can be returned to what was once a healthy way of life. Most members of the general public hold a pessimistic attitude toward therapeutic attempts at restoring any criminal, especially sex offenders. Describing the public's stance, Karl Menninger wrote:

> We don't love criminals. We hate them. We despise them. We regard them as disagreeable, dangerous failures. And we do not really believe, most of us, that they can be rehabilitated, that they can change for the better, or that it is worthwhile making the effort. (1966, p. 242-43).

To go against the grain and advocate for the treatment of sex offenders is a lonely mission. Much of the time we argue on behalf of restorative efforts with little more than hope to support us. Yet it is my firm conviction that therapy can restore offenders to a more humane existence.

Fay Honey Knopp (1992) spoke to the implications of the word "restorative" itself when she said:

> ... 'restorative' fills a yearning, a promise of the way we would like things to be, a moving away from the punishment model, the retributive paradigm that has pervaded public policy, the media and, as a result, our political and cultural direction for so many years.

Many people fear there is a dangerous naïveté underlying the optimism of humanistic psychologists, therapists, and social workers. Sometimes that contention is true. Yet longitudinal studies now reveal encouraging findings concerning the treatability of sex offenders (Freeman-Longo & Blanchard, 1998). The work of Dr. Frank Valcour (1991) further suggests that when comprehensive and eclectic grace-based programming is in place, lasting change does occur. Facilities like St. Luke's Institute of Maryland have found that even fixated pedophiles, long branded as "untreatable," rarely reoffend when comprehensive treatment planning, including relapse prevention, addiction-oriented treatments, cognitive strategies, behavioral techniques, drug interventions, spiritual modalities, and psychodynamic supportive therapies (to name just a few approaches) are used.

Yet, contradicting this encouraging information was the confusing research study out of Minnesota ("Incest offenders," 1991). In that study, sexual offenders were found to benefit very little from psychological treatment. In fact, rapists who completed psychological forms of treatment showed a 40% higher re-arrest rate than the untreated rapists four years after leaving prison. Child molesters who received treatment were almost as likely to be arrested for a sexual crime within four years of leaving prison as untreated molesters. After seven years, they were more likely to be rearrested than the untreated child molesters.

What explains the supposed difference in treatment success of St. Luke's Institute and the Minnesota penal system survey? It may have something to do with variations in the comprehensive nature of the treatment offered, differences between the populations treated, and disparities in the quality of post-release supervision provided.

Traditionally, prisons are not known for their state-of-the-art treatment programs. They also do not provide the kind of compassionate support found in private residential facilities. If this is true, the main contention of this book remains valid: thorough and humanistic treatment can work.

But what of the finding that in some cases psychological treatment was less effective than none at all? One can only speculate about the reasons for this anomaly. Could it be that the minority of sex offenders who make their way to prison are more seriously disturbed and therefore, less treatable? Could it be that treatment provided in a prison environment is not designed to significantly enhance self-esteem? Could it also be that hardened criminals tend to use new-found insights to excuse what they think and do? That for some men, knowledge is not therapeutic but, in fact, is a dangerous thing? Finally, could it be that prison populations are disproportionately comprised of African-Americans who are treated differently (through the use of discriminant sentencing and parole criteria) by the penal system, as Thompson and Smith (1993) contend? The answer to all of these questions, I believe, is yes.

Opposing Treatment Camps

Many helping professionals want to believe that there is a right way and a wrong way to treat sex offenders — a neat prescription that will have perfect application to all types of offenders. Many times our own investment in a treatment program fosters competitive jealousy toward practitioners who use a different model. Behaviorists often disagree with psychodynamic therapists. Proponents of addiction models are often at odds with the traditional psychiatric/ medical model. Practitioners in each sub-field appear to have a vested interest in defending their methods. I believe a comprehensive treatment approach that borrows from different philosophies and is tailored to each offender's unique needs usually will produce the best results.

The overriding theme of this book stresses a humanistic implementation of the individually selected treatment approach. I share the optimism of pioneering humanists like Rogers, Maslow, Adler, and others. The basic tenets espoused by the leaders of the humanist movement rely most on "people skills" and ethical principles to guide the therapeutic process.

While the adherents of competing schools of thought continue their debates, some areas of agreement appear to be emerging. Many experts are now acknowledging the compulsive or addictive features observed in the majority of sex offenders. Most believe control, rather than cure, is the most realistic goal of treatment. Increasingly, more therapists are open to adjunctive Twelve Step recovery models that include spirituality components.

While many practitioners disagree on which should come first — a change in attitude or a change in behavior — everyone seems to agree that both cognitive and behavioral therapies are necessary to bring about change.

Today, members of the helping professions are sensing that while behavior modification techniques do accomplish short-term change, these are, by themselves, a rather simplistic way to treat a very complex problem. Multi-modal approaches are favored.

Disagreement still remains over the importance of investigating issues of causation with sex offenders. On one side, reality therapy proponent William Glasser (1965) has said, "Knowledge of cause has nothing to do with therapy" (p. 53). Glasser's reality therapy always places the focus on the present, with little tolerance for historical data that could be used to excuse unhealthy conduct.

The other side of this argument is well articulated by Carnes (1991) and Schwartz (1992). Carnes argues that each person with a sexual addiction problem must face the fundamental issues that made him vulnerable to addiction in the first place; often, they involve childhood maltreatment and personal shame. Schwartz also sees compulsive sexuality as having its origin in early traumatic experiences surrounding sexual development. A recent trend in therapy with sexual compulsives is to address past issues — often using an abreactive approach that requires "reliving" painful early-life traumas, successfully confronting them, and integrating the experiences into their lives.

Feminists are attempting to influence the helping professions to pay more serious attention to society's tacit approval of sex offending. Their goal is to expand treatment from a narrow individual focus to embrace broader cultural change. While the respective therapeutic camps all pay lip service to this philosophy, little has been done to translate the theories into a pragmatic plan for social reform. At the same time, some clinicians feel pressured to subscribe to feminist theories that have yet to be empirically demonstrated. Again, politics, rightly or wrongly, can push science aside.

Restoring sex offenders to a condition of respect for all of humanity requires Americans, particularly men, to participate in similar restorative efforts that create a cultural climate of change and growth. Treating only the symptom of a problem — sex offending — is to ignore the fertile ground from which much interpersonal violence springs: our violence-loving culture. Rossetti (1990) in his book Slayer of the Soul, eloquently makes this point. He writes:

> Though we may not be individually guilty of the crime of sexual abuse, as a community we are not only responsible for the good that springs from our midst, we are also responsible for the vile as well. We are the seedbed from which such pathology is born. (p. 196)

Restoration, it would follow, must include treatment of the offender, as well as of the pathological environment within which he developed. Removing the cultural supports for sexual abuse is essential to eliminate this public health epidemic. To move in that direction there are many steps we can take. For example:

- Men can confront other men who use sexually insensitive humor, make offensive remarks about women, or utter depersonalizing comments. Radio and television public service announcements could be developed patterned after the

"Friends Don't Let Friends Drive Drunk" spots, which model intervening behavior.

- We can begin education and values clarification as early as elementary school. Some elementary schools are conducting empathy courses that develop healthy gender awareness at an early age. Other schools have instituted sexual harassment education and prevention programs for children.
- We can support fathers in discussing and modeling gender equality before their children. We can teach nonviolent values, reduced competitiveness, and healthy sexuality to our sons.
- We can educate the public about the real dangers of pornography in "fueling the fire" in men who are predisposed to sexually assault (Rosenberg, 1989) with the knowledge that prohibition will not be as effective as open discussion, education, and understanding can be.
- We can educate parents on the early detection of sexual aggressiveness in their young and adolescent children. We can inform parents and health care providers of the vital need for parental therapeutic involvement when any minor is being treated for sexually assaultive behavior.
- We can insist on mandatory training for judges on the nature and treatment of sex offending. While opposing information exists even within the helping professions, a well-informed judge who can understand all sides of an issue can best respond to the problem of sex offending.
- We can implement broad and sweeping prison reform. Offender programs must be well funded, state-of-the-art, and preferably, segregated by crime.
- We can dramatically reduce media depictions of sexual violence, sexism, objectification, and stereotypically narrow gender assignments.
- We can educate helping professionals regarding their own emotional vulnerabilities and how these wounds, if left unattended, can contribute to sexually exploitive client relations. We can introduce university curriculum changes

that better prepare helping professionals for the sexual dilemmas they will eventually face in their practices.

- We can educate the public on the danger of sexual exploitation in their relationships with helping professionals and provide advocacy programs that supportively guide victims through encounters with boards of medicine, licensing boards, and so on.
- We can develop community restorative justice programs such as those in Canada and New Zealand. Family conferencing programs can be instituted that focus more on healing and restoration than on punishment (Church Council on Justice and Corrections, 1996).

I keep my ideals because in spite of everything I still believe that people are really good at heart. I simply can't build up my hopes on a foundation consisting of confusion, misery and death. I can feel the sufferings of millions, and yet, if I look up into the heavens, I think that it will come right, that this cruelty too will end, and that peace and tranquility will return again.

— Anne Frank
(quoted in Larson & Micheels-Cyrus, 1987, p. 263)

CHAPTER 6

Compassionate Therapy

The son of a bitch that did this [sexual molestation] to that little girl should be castrated with a rusty knife! Really, the pervert doesn't even deserve to live!

— anonymous patient (personal communication, 1993)

When we look beneath the surface, beneath the impulsive evil deed, we see within our enemy-neighbor a measure of goodness and know that the viciousness and evilness of his acts are not quite representative of all that he is. We see him in a new light.

— Martin Luther King, Jr. (1963, p. 49)

THE THERAPEUTIC RELATIONSHIP is central to any counseling process. When the therapist's empathy, respect, and concern for the sex offender are evident, and when the offender feels understood and empowered and has not become inappropriately dependent on the therapist, he will be less hesitant to become involved in meaningful therapy (Derlega, Hendrick, Winstead, & Berg, 1991). The establishment of this type of caring relationship early in therapy will be crucial for a successful outcome (Malan, 1976). To practice this formula for success, every therapist must examine his/her prejudices, filters, dislikes, and outside influences to guarantee they will not contaminate the relationship.

Referring the sex offender to a healthy therapist skilled in the use of self will foster treatment success more predictably than the use of any specific technique. The qualities found in effective therapists almost always include the elements of congruence, authenticity, warmth, equality, vulnerability, humor, and compassion.

Congruence

Carl Rogers (1951, 1961a, 1961b) enumerated three basic attitudes, all quite similar, that he believed were important to the success of therapy: the therapist's congruence, authenticity, and genuineness.

Congruence refers to the consistent manner in which we present as we feel, say what we mean, and act in accordance with the values we espouse. Being reliable and honest is critical in making a connection with any person, but it is especially so with a sex offender. Hardly anyone is better at spotting a sham or a phony than a man who himself has led a life of crime and dishonesty. Criminals will not respect a counselor who is duplicitous or masks large parts of himself or herself while demanding rigorous honesty from his clients. The very nature of conducting treatment with a sex offender puts the therapist in the position of being a role model.

Congruence could sound like this:

I just noticed that I wasn't telling you exactly how I feel about your reoffense. Actually, I was very saddened by all the people who were hurt by it — yourself included. That is probably what you were seeing on my face.

Authenticity

To be authentic is to be genuine. An individual who is genuine can be spontaneous, true-to-life, and therefore, trustworthy. Rogers (quoted in Baldwin, 1987) believes that the fully authentic therapist must first feel completely secure as an individual. If the therapist cannot be himself or herself, neither can his or her clients. This quality of presence suggests that the therapist is being totally forthright and personally available to the offender.

For years the sex offender may have worn a mask that falsely projected masculinity, security, competency, virility, and power, while he privately felt unmanly, insecure, incompetent, impotent, and powerless. "Getting real" always felt threatening to him. However, when a therapist can model an authentic presence, and empathy, along with confidence and security, a transformation in the offender is likely to occur.

Authenticity comes through in this therapeutic comment in a situation where both client and therapist are frustrated by the lack of continued progress:

> *Sometimes I wish I had more insights than I do. It's frustrating for me to tell you I don't have all the answers. You still will get my best shot and I believe that's worth a good deal.*

Warmth

Warmth does not necessarily indicate weakness, although many rapists have told me they initially believed it did. A history of childhood abuse without consistent and dependable expressions of warmth is in the background of most sex offenders. Their early-life narcissistic wounds often were the result of psychological maltreatment, emotional neglect, abandonment, or shaming experiences. Negative attachment experiences and a lack of bonding are not uncommon. With that kind of history, they would naturally suspect any demonstration of warmth. Offenders may see it as disingenuous, a technique designed to trick them. Nevertheless, warmth must first be experienced if it is ever to be given.

Combined with naïveté, a therapist's warmth can easily be manipulated by an offender for his own ends (to circumvent treatment rules, for example). But when offered from a posture of strength, that warmth diminishes power struggles and many of the adversarial factors that can develop in a counseling relationship.

Warmth is what Perlman (1979, p. 206) referred to as compassionate responsiveness — the essential ingredient for the nourishment of our emotional and spiritual development.

Warmth, offered from a position of strength, may sound like this:

It appears you are in a lot of pain right now as you prepare to make your police statement. I'll accompany you through this experience and give you as much support as I can. We must go now, however, and do what needs to be done. Let's talk to the officer.

Equality

A natural power imbalance exists between any helping professional and his/her clients. Clients and therapists are not (and should not be) equal in all ways. This imbalance often feels threatening to sex offenders. They are not inclined to enter into any social encounter that leaves them feeling "one-down" or at a disadvantage.

Many therapists use threats when they believe some clout is needed to gain an offender's compliance. This can be a tactical mistake that frequently stymies client cooperation. Offenders recognize our power and respect us most when we can "sit on it." Lowering authority, as it is called, is most effective when used in response to the offender's observable therapeutic participation. It is, however, okay to use our power for constructive ends (for example, to help set limits, for therapeutic confrontations, and so on). But power is most helpful when it is conspicuously left in its holster.

Acknowledging the offender as a valued partner in the change process also demonstrates equality. Inviting him to brainstorm with us, set goals with us, and participate in progress evaluations shows equality. And equality gives rise to therapeutic engagement.

Equality may be communicated this way:

I'm going to need to hear more from you in our sessions. There isn't going to be much progress without more input from you. Let's put our heads together and see if we can do some effective work. I value your ideas.

Such a statement must, however, then be followed by a real commitment to the offender's participation, and the authentic listening to and welcoming of the offender's ideas.

Vulnerability

All of us are emotionally raw at times. We know it and offenders know it. There is no sense in hiding it. A constant effort to conceal our vulnerabilities encourages the offender to respond in kind. When, however, the therapist is willing to judiciously self-disclose, his credibility — and therefore, his influence — is enhanced.

Miller and Baldwin (1987) write, "We believe that conscious inner attention to one's wounds and conflicts leads to a sense of vulnerability. This in turn makes possible the unconscious connection between the healer's wound and the patient's healer ..." (p. 147). Jung's position was even more strongly stated. He believed that only the wounded doctor could heal. That position might be tempered somewhat by the caveat that *untreated* wounded healers can be quite dangerous (Blanchard & Irons, 1993).

Awareness of our wounds is important. Accepting them and healing them adds to the therapist's wholeness. This in turn enables the sex offender to attempt to do the same.

A careful expression of the therapist's vulnerability can be shared in this fashion:

Today is one of those days when you guys in the offender group have shown me I have a few control issues of my own to look at. Thanks!

Humor

The last thing the general public would have us do by way of treatment is to imply to sex offenders that their crimes are taken lightly. In fact, most people seem hard-pressed to appreciate how humor could play any role in an offender's recovery plan. We are charged by society with the responsibility of hating these men and their acts. From that stance there is certainly no room for laughter in the counseling office.

Typically, offenders have led very unhappy, unbalanced lives. Because they regard the world as a perpetual threat to their safety and happiness, sex offenders are uncomfortable letting down their guard. Theirs is a humorless existence. These are fractured men without any sense of wholeness. Many grew up too fast and only infrequently, if ever, enjoyed the gaiety and playfulness of childhood. Humor, to them, was often expressed only at the expense of others.

Humor has its place in the therapeutic setting. When used properly it is not about joke-telling. Rather, humor is the natural extension of an authentic and healthy personality. A combination of high tension and an occasionally playful spirit can inject a sudden sparkle of humorous intimacy into therapy.

A lighthearted tease or a playful sally works best from a foundation of trust. Used sporadically, this type of humor can strengthen the therapeutic bond. It implies acceptance. Healthy and respectful humor is experienced by the offender as an invitation to be personal. It can take the edge of tension away from many a stressful situation and enable the therapist to confront the offender more easily without being annihilating. Humor also helps sex offenders be more open to our advice. Men in this climate will reveal far more information than they will in a session where the therapist browbeats or shames them.

Perhaps one of the least tangible, yet most valuable, features of therapeutic humor is its ability to impart hope. Hope is the carrot that, when matched with the offender's ever-present pain, motivates him to change.

A playful exchange may be the "sugar that helps the medicine go down." For example:

OFFENDER: *I understand you want me to be seen by another psychologist. Is this really necessary?*

THERAPIST: *I believe it is — two heads are better than one here. Getting a second opinion from a neuropsychologist could prove to be quite helpful in your case.*

OFFENDER (wryly): *You counselors must make a fortune off us guys.*

THERAPIST (smiling): *Hey, we all need another new sports car from time to time.*

OFFENDER: *Are you serious?*

THERAPIST: *Only about what is best for you.*

OFFENDER (in a conciliatory tone): *All right. I'll go along with the referral. I guess you haven't let me down yet. But I will get a ride in that new car, right?*

THERAPIST (laughing): *You will be the first!*

Compassion

It is understandable that the public (and even some therapists) would be so averse to any displays of mercy or charity toward sex offenders. After all, these violent and abusive men have ripped apart the lives of many innocent citizens, including our wives, sisters, children, and friends. Those of us in the helping professions who are primarily responsible for the treatment of sexual violence must somehow appreciate the level of emotion generated by the damage sexual abuse wreaks and still be objective observers of its etiology and proponents of its most practical remedies.

The kind of compassion being called for is not a maudlin sympathy, nor is it approval of a man's assaultive behavior. It is a willingness to attempt understanding of the sex offender's emotional condition and life situation with a concern for his growth and happiness. At times, a compassionate therapist will be unequivocally moralistic, but never shaming.

Compassion can be conveyed in a firm and critical tone while still being received as an expression of kindness and concern. Compassion can be delivered tacitly by one's willingness to persevere over time as the offender still clings to unhealthy defense mechanisms such as denial, rationalization, or minimization. Compassion can be seen in the therapist's consistent honesty with the offender, even when he is tempted to be otherwise. This kind of compassion is sometimes referred to as "tough love."

Tough love can be communicated to the offender in this way:

There is no doubt about it. You have made some serious mistakes choosing to be sexual with your daughter. The pain you are now feeling is deserved and necessary; it is a part of the recovery process to be in touch with these emotions. It must be difficult for your entire family as well. I care enough about you to let you live with that pain for now. It will eventually lift and I'll still be at your side then.

Certain counseling tenets have stood the test of experience. The solid principles of the humanist philosophy apply to all clients — sex offenders included. Of those cherished tenets and principles, the use of self in the therapeutic relationship offers the greatest promise for restoring the lives of sex offenders. If we truly desire to protect our citizenry, we must choose strategies of treatment that have been shown to work. A reactionary treatment response marked by vengeance and punishment may make its proponents feel good in the moment, but it leaves many Americans in continued danger when the sex offender is again back on the street.

Revengeful feelings only escalate bitterness. Disrespect works similarly. A tough love approach balances compassion with swift and stern consequences. Kottler (1992) in a remarkably insightful book, *Compassionate Therapy*, writes, "Every client wants to feel valued and understood by us; it is when we trade our compassion for cynicism that we lose the opportunity to be helpful" (p. 187).

Sex offenders become difficult and resistant when we fail to connect with them on a respectful, humane level. Compassion, firm values, and a respectful authority (not to be confused with authoritarianism) create lasting therapeutic results. These are the results that protect our loved ones.

In our every deliberation, we must consider the impact of our decisions on the next seven generations ... on those faces that are yet beneath the ground.

— The Great Law of the Six Nations, Iroquois Confederacy
(Quoted in Larson & Micheels-Cyrus, 1987, p. 118)

Conclusion

WITHIN EVERY MAN who has committed a sex offense, there is an issue ready to enlighten us — the helpers and the public. Whether it be fear, insecurity, anger, power, or control, these are the issues confounding today's men. The offender has progressed further along a continuum of sexual mistreatment than most of us. We may, however, be on the same path. As is said in Twelve Step recovery circles, "There but for the grace of God go I." Like the miner's canary, the sex offender announces the illness of our society, our national family. As a large family system, the ill health of one member reflects the entire system's dysfunction. As one person falls, he sounds a warning to the rest of us. We must heed it.

When we distance ourselves from our vulnerabilities by disclaiming them, the cycle of abuse goes on. When we regard sex offenders as a very different breed of men, the climate for oppression goes unchallenged. If we instead embrace the struggle that is common to us all, we can take a step toward creating a climate of nonviolence and mutual high regard.

The change process involved in restoring sex offenders involves a reciprocal energy. Group therapy creates a climate of rigorous honesty and revelation that can be contagious to all the offenders and facilitators alike. Anyone experienced in this type of group work knows of the good feelings that resonate among all brave people who collectively risk exposure on the road to growth.

Jonas Robitscher, author of *The Powers of Psychiatry* (1980), formulated a maxim that succinctly describes effective individual therapy. He said, "Good therapy is an engagement of two people that leaves both changed. If only the patient changes, the therapy has been a failure" (p. 488).

Our own happiness rests in part with our willingness to grow in the ways these troubled men are subtly guiding us. To hear of their pain and to be a part of their change process can enrich the life of the therapist. We must be willing to recognize our collective humanity and attempt to connect with all people if we are to create a safer society.

So it is that the helper who is open and resonant to the lives of others is himself the recipient of a variegated and expanded life experience. This is no small reward, that our inner world becomes enlivened and enriched by our relationships with so many different human beings in so many different life situations.

— Helen Perlman (1979, p. 206)

You cannot shake hands with a clenched fist.

— Indira Gandhi
(Quoted in Peacemaking: Day to Day, 1985, p. 127)

References

Andrews, F. (1991). *The art and practice of loving*. New York: St. Martins.

Aponte, H., & Winter, J. (1987). The person and practice of the therapist: Treatment and training. In M. Baldwin & V. Satir (Eds.), *The use of self in therapy* (pp. 85-111). New York: Haworth.

Baldwin, M. (1987). Interview with Carl Rogers on the use of self in therapy. In M. Baldwin & V. Satir (Eds.), *The use of self in therapy* (pp. 45-52). New York: Haworth.

Baldwin, M., & Satir, V. (Eds.) (1987). *The use of self in therapy*. New York: Haworth.

Bazelon, D. (November, 1961). *Equal justice for the unequal*. Lecture 3 of the American Psychiatric Association, Isaac Ray Lectureship Award Series.

Blanchard, G.T. (1990). Differential diagnosis of sex offenders: Distinguishing characteristics of the sex addict. *American Journal of Preventive Psychiatry and Neurology, 2*(3), 45-47.

Blanchard, G.T., & Irons, R. (1993, December). The sexually assaultive helping professional: Profiling child molesters. Paper presented at the *Sixth National Conference on Child Abuse and Neglect*, Pittsburgh, PA.

Briere, J.N. (1992). *Child abuse trauma*. Newbury Park, CA: Sage.

Briere, J.N., & Runtz, M. (1989). University males' sexual interest in children: Predicting potential indices of pedophilia in a non-forensic sample. *Child Abuse and Neglect, 13*, 65-75.

Burket, E., & Bruni, F. (1992). *A gospel of shame*. New York: Viking.

Carnes, P. (1983). *Out of the shadows*. Minneapolis: CompCare.

Carnes, P. (1989). *Contrary to love*. Minneapolis: CompCare.

Carnes, P. (1991). *Don't call it love*. New York: Bantam.

Church Council on Justice and Corections. (1996). *Satisfying justice*. Ottawa, ONT, Canada: Author.

Clark, R. (1970). *Crime in America*. New York: Simon & Schuster.

Collier, H.V. (1987). The differing self: Women as psychotherapists. In M. Baldwin & V. Satir (Eds.), *The use of self in therapy* (pp. 53-60). New York: Haworth.

Courtemanche, M. (December, 1982). Innate criminality revisted. *Canada's Mental Health*, 25-26.

Derlega, V., Hendrick, S., Winstead, B., & Berg, J. (1991). *Psychotherapy as a personal relationship*. New York: Guilford.

deShazer, S. (1984). The death of resistance. *Family process, 23* (1), 11-17.

Doherty, W. (1995). *Soul searching: Why psychotherapy must promote moral responsibility*. New York: Basic Books.

Fine, R. (1985). Countertransference reactions to the difficult patient. In Strean, H. (Ed.), *Psychoanalytic approaches to the resistant client* (pp. 7-22). New York: Haworth.

Finkelhor, D., & Lewis, I. A. (1988). An epidemiologic approach to the study of child molestation. In R. Prentky & V. Quinsey (Eds.), *Human sexual aggression: Current perspectives* (pp. 64-78). New York: Annals of the New York Academy of Sciences.

Freeman-Longo, R.E., & Blanchard, G. (1998). *Sexual abuse in America: Epidemic of the 21st century*. Brandon, VT: Safer Society.

Gardner, R. (1991). *Sex abuse hysteria: Salem witch trials revisited*. Cresskill, NJ: Creative Therapeutics.

Gilligan, J. (1996). *Violence: Our deadly epidemic and its causes*. New York: Grosset/Putnam.

Gillin, J.L. (1931). *Taming the criminal*. New York: Macmillan.

Glasser, W. (1965). *Reality therapy*. New York: Harper.

Greenson, R. (1987). Resistance analysis. In D. Milman & G. Goldman, (Eds.), *Techniques of working with resistance*. (pp. 133-166). Northvale, NJ: Jason Aronson.

Groth, A.N. (1983). *Juvenile and adult sex offenders: Creating a community response*. Lecture sponsored by the Tompkins County Sexual Abuse Task Force, Ithaca, New York.

Halleck, S. (1967). *Psychiatry and dilemmas of crime*. New York: Harper & Row.

Herman, J.L. (1988). Considering sex offenders: A model of addiction. *Signs: Journal of Women in Culture and Society, 12*(4), 695-724.

Hylton, J.H. (September 1981). Innate criminality revisited. *Canada's Mental Health*, 12-26.

Incest offenders are usually sent to treatment. (Analysis, November 10, 1991). *Minneapolis Star Tribune*, p. 1A.

King, M.L. (1963). *Strength to love*. Philadelphia: Fortress.

Knopp, F.H. (1984) *Retraining adult sex offenders: Methods and models*. Orwell, VT: Safer Society.

Knopp, F.H. (November, 1992). *Restorative justice for juvenile sex offenders*. Speech to the National Council of Juvenile and Family Court Judges. Lake Tahoe/Reno, NV.

Knopp, F.H.; Freeman-Longo, R.E.; & Stevenson, W.F. (1992). *Nationwide survey of juvenile and adult sex offender treatment programs and models, 1992*. Orwell, VT: Safer Society.

Kottler, J. (1992). *Compassionate therapy*. San Francisco: Jossey-Bass.

Kraxiec, R. (May, 1990). "Silent shame." *Pittsburgh*, p. 51.

Larson, J., & Micheels-Cyrus, M. (Eds.). (1987). *Seeds of peace*. Philadephia: New Society.

Lazarus, A.A., & Fay, A. (1982). Resistance or rationalization? A cognitive-behavioral perspective. In P. L. Wachtel (Ed.), *Resistance: Psychodynamic and behavioral approaches* (pp. 115-132). New York: Plenum.

Malamuth, N. M. (Fall, 1985). Media's new mood: Sexual violence. (Interview). *Media and values*, 33: 3-5.

Malan, D. H. (1976). *The frontier of brief psychotherapy: An example of the convergence of research and clinical practice*. New York: Plenum.

Maletzky, B. (1991). *Treating the sexual offender*. Newbury Park, CA: Sage.

Maslow, A. (1962). *Toward a psychology of being*. New York: Van Nostrand Reinhold.

Menninger, K. (1966). *The crime of punishment*. New York: Viking.

Miller, G. D., & Baldwin, D.W.C. (1987). Implications of the wounded-healer paradigm for the use of the self in therapy. *Journal of Psychotherapy & the Family*, *3*(1), 139-151.

Murphy, J., & Dison, J. (1990). *Are prisons any better?* Newbury Park, CA: Sage.

Peacemaking: Day to day. (1985). Erie, PA: Pax Christi USA.

Perlman, H.H. (1979). *Relationship.* Chicago: University of Chicago.

Plyer, A., Woolley, C., & Anderson, T. (1990). Current treatment providers. In A. Horton, B. Johnson, L. Roundy, & Williams, D. (Eds.), *The incest perpetrator* (pp. 198-218). Newbury Park, CA: Sage.

Robitscher, J. (1980). *The powers of psychiatry.* Boston: Houghton Mifflin.

Rogers, C. (1951). *Client-centered therapy.* Boston: Houghton-Mifflin.

Rogers, C. (1961a). The process equation of psychotherapy. *American Journal of Psychotherapy, 14,* 27-45.

Rogers, C. (1961b). *On becoming a person.* Boston: Houghton Mifflin.

Rosenberg, J. (1989). *Fuel on the fire: An inquiry into "pornography" & sexual aggression in a free society.* Orwell, VT: Safer Society.

Rossetti, S. (Ed.) (1990). *Slayer of the soul.* Mystic, CT: Twenty-Third.

Russell, J. (1993). *Out of bounds.* Newbury Park, CA: Sage.

Samenow, S. (1984). *Inside the criminal mind.* New York: Times Books.

Sanday, P. R. (1981). *Female power and male dominance: On the origins of sexual equality.* London: Cambridge University.

Satir, V., & Baldwin, M. (1983). *Satir step by step.* Palo Alto, CA: Science & Behavior.

Schwartz, M. (June 1992). Sexual compulsivity as post-traumatic stress disorder: Treatment perspectives. *Psychiatric Annals, 22*(6), 333-338.

Smiljanich, K. (1992). University students' self-reported sexual interest in children. Unpublished master's thesis, California State University, Dominguez Hills.

Storring, V. (Producer). (1991, November 12). "My doctor, my lover." *Frontline.* Washington, DC: Public Broadcasting System:

Strean, H., & Freeman, L. (1993). *Our wish to kill.* New York: Avon.

Thompson, V.L.S., & Smith, S.D.W. (1993). Attitudes of African American adults toward treatment in cases of child sexual abuse. *Journal of Child Sexual Abuse, 2*(1), 5-19.

Valcour, F. (May 20, 1991). Speech to the National Conference on Sexual Compulsivity and Addiction. San Francisco, CA.

Warren, R., & Green, M. (1997). The new transformative treatment paradigm (TTP): A response to interpersonal sexual aggression in an unsafe society. *Sexual Addiction & Compulsivity, 4*(1), 43-67.

Warrensford, D. (1990, March 7). Sex offenders deserve banishment, surgery. *USA Today*, p. 11A.

Washington state senate OKs castration bill. (1990, January 28). *Billings* (Montana) *Gazette*, p. 2.

Webster's new dictionary and thesaurus (Concise ed.). (1990). New York: Russell, Geddes & Grossett

Whitaker, C. A., & Malone, T. P. (1953). *The roots of psychotherapy.* New York: Blakiston.

Yalom, I. (1980). *Existential psychotherapy.* New York: Basic Books.

Yochelson, S., & Samenow, S. (1986). *The criminal personality, Vol. II: The change process.* Northvale, NJ: Jason Aronson.

"This volume will serve as an important and comprehensive tool for journalists — or anyone — looking into the compelling and urgent issues surrounding sexual abuse in America."

— Elizabeth Karnes
Long-time researcher for
Bill Moyers, PBS and
CBS News

ISBN # 1-884444-45-8

224 pages, paper

Price $20.00

Order # WP058

$2.00 from every copy of *Sexual Abuse In America* sold is dedicated to child sexual abuse prevention.

Sexual Abuse in America:
Epidemic of the 21ˢᵗ Century.

by Robert E. Freeman-Longo and Geral T. Blanchard

Offering a new and unique perspective, *Sexual Abuse in America* is important reading for anyone interested in understanding and preventing sexual abuse. With more than 45 years of sexual abuse treatment and prevention experience, the authors profile sexual abuse in American society, discuss abusive sexuality as a public health epidemic, and outline how Americans can prevent sexual abuse from recurring.

Despite the epidemic increase in incidence of sexual abuse, government at all levels has refused to recognize and treat it as a public health issue requiring prevention as well as treatment. Instead legislators are spending increasing (and increasingly scarce) tax dollars on ill-conceived legislation enacting punitive measures that may be making the sexual abuse problem worse. *Sexual Abuse in America* describes:

- How the various media contribute to the sexual abuse problem in America.
- How the news media's reporting on sexual crimes often misinforms the public.
- How the sex-for-sale industries abuse human sexuality and contribute to the sexual abuse problem in America.
- Why current "feel good" legislation such a "Megan's Law" and "Chemical Castration" laws are ineffective in preventing sexual abuse, and why they may be contributing to worsening the sexual abuse problem in America.
- Current sexual abuse prevention strategies and their effectiveness.
- Proposed sexual abuse prevention strategies for the 21st Century.

"At last the book that exposes what the media and those who would use the tragedy of sexual abuse to serve their own needs has been written. Not until public policy relies on research findings and places the healing of the victim, the community and the abuser as its priority will this national crisis be addressed. Freeman-Longo and Blanchard have presented an impassioned call to this mission in their volume. It should be in the library of every person charged with promoting public safety."

—Barbara K. Schwartz, Ph.D.
Clinical Director, Justice Resource Institute

1998 The Safer Society Press (802)247-3132

Selected
Safer Society
Publications

Back on Track: Boys Dealing with Sexual Abuse by Leslie Bailey Wright and Mindy Loiselle (1997). A workbook for boys ages 10 and up. Foreword by David Calof. $14. WP056

Shining Through: Pulling It Together After Sexual Abuse SECOND EDITION by Leslie Bailey Wright and Mindy Loiselle (1997). A workbook for girls ages 10 and up. $16. WP052

STOP! Just for Kids: For Kids with Sexual Touching Problems Adapted by Terri Allred and Gerald Burns from original writings of children in a treatment program (1997). $15. WP051

When Children Abuse: Group Treatment Strategies for Children with Impulse Control Problems by Carolyn Cunningham and Kee MacFarlane (1996). $28. WP041

Tell It Like It Is: A Resource for Youth in Treatment by Alice Tallmadge with Galyn Forster (1998). Interviews with teens in treatment for sexually abusive behavior. $15. WP059

The Relapse Prevention Workbook for Youth in Treatment by Charlene Steen (1993). $18. WP022

Pathways: A Guided Workbook for Youth Beginning Treatment by Timothy J. Kahn (Revised Edition 2001). $22. WP090

Pathways Guide for Parents of Youth Beginning Treatment by Timothy J. Kahn (Revised Edition 1997) $8. WP057

Mother-Son Incest: The Unthinkable Broken Taboo — An Overview of Findings by Hani Miletski (1995). $10. WP045

Man-to-Man, When Your Partner Says NO: Pressured Sex & Date Rape by Scott A. Johnson (1992). $8. WP008

From Trauma to Understanding: A Guide for Parents of Children with Sexual Behavior Problems by William D. Pithers, Alison S. Gray, Carolyn Cunningham, & Sandy Lane (1993). $5. WP021

Adolescent Sexual Offender Assessment Packet by Alison Stickrod Gray & Randy Wallace (1992). $8. WP011

Sexual Abuse in America: Epidemic of the 21st Century by Robert E. Freeman-Longo & Geral T. Blanchard (1998). $20. WP058

Personal Sentence Completion Inventory by L.C. Miccio-Fonseca, PhD (1998). $50, includes 25 inventories and user's guide. Additional inventories available in packs of 25 for $25. WP048

When You Don't Know Who to Call: A Consumer's Guide to Selecting Mental Health Care by Nancy Schaufele & Donna Kennedy (1998). $15. WP060

Assessing Sexual Abuse: A Resource Guide for Practitioners edited by Robert Prentky and Stacey Bird Edmunds (1997). $25. WP050

Impact. Working with Sexual Abusers editied by Stacey Bird Edmunds (1997). $20. WP042

The Difficult Connection: The Therapeutic Relationship in Sex Offender Treatment by Geral T. Blanchard (1998). $12. WP028

Supervision of the Sex Offender by Georgia Cumming and Maureen Buell (1997). $25. WP053

A Primer on the Complexities of Traumatic Memories of Childhood Sexual Abuse: A Psychobiological Approach by Fay Honey Knopp & Anna Rose Benson (1997). $20. WP043

The Last Secret: Daughters Sexually Abused by Mothers by Bobbie Rosencrans (1997). $20. WP046

When Your Wife Says No: Forced Sex in Marriage by Fay Honey Knopp (1994). $7. WP024

Female Adolescent Sexual Abusers: An Exploratory Study of Mother-Daughter Dynamics with Implications for Treatment by Marcia T. Turner & Tracey N. Turner (1994). $18. WP027

Adult Sexual Offender Assessment Packet prepared by Mark Carich & Donya Adkerson (1995). $8. WP029

Because There Is A Way To Prevent Child Sexual Guide edited by Joan Tabachnick (1998). $1. (Bulk discount available) Min. Order of 10 WP071 Available in Spanish 35¢ - Min. Order of 10 WP087

Do Children Sexually Abuse Other Children edited by Joan Tabachnick (1999). 50¢ Min. Order of 10 WP075

Healthy Thinking/Feeling/Doing by Jack Pransky and Lori Carpenos (2000). $28. WP073

SOS Help for Emotions Managing Anxiety, Anger, & Depression by Lynn Clark, Ph. D. (1998) $13.50 WP080

But He Says He Loves Me: Girls Speaking Out on Dating Abuse by Nicole B. Sperekas, Ph. D. (2002) $15. WP079

Handbook of Sexual Abuse Assesment and Treatment by Mark S. Carich, Ph. D. & Steven E. Mussack, Ph. D. (2001) $28. WP083

Adult Relapse Prevention Workbook by Charlene Steen, Ph. D. (2001) $22. WP085

What's Happening In Our Family: Understanding Sexual Abuse Through Metaphors by Constance M. Ostis, M.S.W. (2002) $20

The Safer Society Press is a program of The Safer Society Foundation, Inc., a 501(c)3 nonprofit national agency dedicated to the prevention and treatment of sexual abuse. To receive a catalog of our complete listings, please check the box on the order form (next page) and mail it to the address listed or call us at (802) 247-3132. For more information on the Safer Society Foundation, Inc., visit our website at http://www.safersociety.org.

Adults Molested As Children: A Survivor's Manual for Women & Men by Euan Bear with Peter Dimock (1988; 4th printing). $12.95.

Family Fallout: A Handbook for Families of Adult Sexual Abuse Survivors by Dorothy Beaulieu Landry, M.Ed. (1991). $12.95.

Embodying Healing: Integrating Bodywork and Psychotherapy in Recovery from Childhood Sexual Abuse by Robert J. Timms, PhD, and Patrick Connors, CMT. (1992). $15.00.

The Safer Society Press is part of The Safer Society Foundation, Inc., a 501(c)3 non-profit agency dedicated to the prevention and treatment of sexual abuse. We publish additional books, audiocassetttes, and training videos related to the treatment of sexual abuse. To receive a catalog of our complete listings, please check the box on the order form (next page) and mail it to the address listed or call us at (802) 247-3132. For more information on the Safer Society Foundation, Inc., visit our website at http://www.safersociety.org.

Safer Press Order Form

Shipping Address: All books shipped via United Parcel Services. Please include a street location for shipping as we can not ship to a Post Office box.		Date:
Name and/or Agency		
Street Address (no P.O. Box):		
City:	State:	Zip:
Daytime Phone:		
Billing Address (if different from shipping address):		
Address:		
City:	State:	Zip:
Daytime Phone:	P.O. #:	
Visa or Master Card #	Exp. Date:	
Signature (for credit card order):		

Qty	Title	Unit Price	Total Cost
☐	Please send me a FREE sample of *Because There Is A way To Prevent Child Abuse* guidebook.	Free	
		Subtotal:	
		VT Residents add 5% sales tax:	
Yes, I want to make a difference through the Safer Society by donating:			
		Shipping (see below):	
All orders must be prepaid		Total:	

Make checks payable to:
SAFER SOCIETY FOUNDATION
All prices subject to change without notice. No returns.

Mail to:
SAFER SOCIETY FOUNDATION
P.O. Box 340
Brandon, VT 05733-0340

Shipping & Handling

1-4 items: $5	26-30 items: $20
5-10 items: $8	31-35 items: $23
11-15 items: $12	36-40 items: $26
16-20 items: $14	41-50 items: $31
21-25 items: $17	Over 50 items: Call for quote

Call for quote on rush orders and for
Alaska & Hawaii orders:
802-247-3132

Phone orders accepted with MasterCard or Visa (call 802-247-3132)